CW00983652

a stream of *stars*

Also by Sangharakshita

A Survey of Buddhism
The Three Jewels
Crossing the Stream
The Essence of Zen
Human Enlightenment
The Religion of Art
The Ten Pillars of Buddhism
The Eternal Legacy
Alternative Traditions
Ambedkar and Buddhism
The History of My Going for Refuge
The Taste of Freedom
New Currents in Western Buddhism
A Guide to the Buddhist Path
Vision and Transformation
The Buddha's Victory
The Rainbow Road *(memoirs)*
Facing Mount Kanchenjunga *(memoirs)*
In the Sign of the Golden Wheel *(memoirs)*
The Drama of Cosmic Enlightenment
Wisdom Beyond Words
The Priceless Jewel
In the Realm of the Lotus

Tibetan Buddhism: An Introduction
Peace is a Fire
The FWBO and 'Protestant Buddhism'
Forty-Three Years Ago
The Meaning of Conversion in Buddhism
Travel Letters
Complete Poems 1941–1994
Was the Buddha a Bhikkhu?
Transforming Self and World
Buddhism for Today – and Tomorrow
Who is the Buddha?
What is the Dharma?
The Inconceivable Emancipation
Ritual and Devotion in Buddhism

Booklets

Extending the Hand of Fellowship
My Relation to the Order
The Meaning of Orthodoxy in Buddhism
Mind – Reactive and Creative
Going for Refuge
Buddhism and the West
Great Buddhists of the Twentieth Century

a stream of

WINDHORSE PUBLICATIONS

stars

reflections and aphorisms

Sangharakshita

Published by Windhorse Publications
11 Park Road, Birmingham, B13 8AB

© Sangharakshita, 1998

Printed by Interprint Ltd, Marsa, Malta
Designed by Dhammarati
Text compiled by Abhaya

Cover image © Photodisc

British Library Cataloguing in Publication Data:
A catalogue record for this book is available from the British Library.

ISBN 1 899579 08 7

CONTENTS

INTRODUCTION

MANY PEOPLE'S FIRST taste of Sangharakshita's interpretation of the Dharma, the teaching of the Buddha, is through his books on Buddhism, or through classes at a centre of the Friends of the Western Buddhist Order, the Buddhist movement that he founded in 1967. Others may have first come across him in a slim collection of sayings and writings entitled *Peace is a Fire*, which appeared almost twenty years ago. Since then he has continued to write and to speak, with great clarity and conviction, on a variety of Buddhist and related topics, generating a steady stream of words that have inspired spiritual change in the lives of thousands of men and women in various parts of the world. It is clearly time for a new anthology.

The impetus to start work on a second collection came when Sangharakshita handed me a neatly written notebook full of unpublished aphorisms and extracts from personal correspondence.

For the rest, I sifted through some of his prodigious output since 1979: mostly literary versions of his talks, as well as several transcripts of study seminars that he conducted in the early eighties.

This new selection reflects the development of Sangharakshita's further thinking on a diversity of topics. He considers the nature of Buddhist tolerance, the danger of charisma, and the relationship between rights and duties, and looks again at various aspects of spiritual development, showing how it extends to the individual's responsibility as citizen, parent, and friend. Open the book at random, and you might come across an aphorism about the Genghis Khan complex, about metaphor as a clue to the nature of reality, or the connection between a sexual relationship and a lobster pot!

The aphorisms, by their very nature, stand by, and speak for, themselves. The rest are excerpts. While they stood out from their context, asking, so to speak, to be chosen, they inevitably lost something in the process of extraction, like jewels loosened from their setting. Hopefully, some readers, sensing this, will feel inspired, where possible, to trace the extracts back to their original context.

Dharmachari Abhaya, Cambridge, August 1997

SANGHARAKSHITA: *A Short Biography*

SANGHARAKSHITA (D.P.E. LINGWOOD) is one of the most prominent Buddhist figures of the second half of the twentieth century. In his teens he read widely in Western literature and comparative religion, and studied whatever Buddhist texts he could get hold of. Two of these, the *Diamond Sutra* and the *Platform Sutra* of the Zen School, had a profound impact on him, convincing him that he was, and always had been, a Buddhist.

After leaving the army in 1945 he remained in India, where he eventually received ordination as a Buddhist monk and studied with several teachers from the major traditions of Buddhism. He established a Buddhist vihara in Kalimpong in the foothills of the Himalayas. There he immersed himself in the study and practice of the Dharma and in teaching. At this time he also wrote what is perhaps his most influential work, *A Survey of Buddhism*.

In 1956, the great social reformer Dr B.R. Ambedkar renounced Hinduism and turned to Buddhism, together with many thousands of his 'Untouchable' followers. Immediately following Ambedkar's sudden death soon after the mass conversions, Sangharakshita played a crucial role in rallying Ambedkar's grief-stricken followers and keeping alive their faith in Buddhism.

After twenty years in India Sangharakshita returned to England and in 1967 set up the Buddhist movement called the Friends of the Western Buddhist Order (FWBO). His work in India was eventually taken up by some of his Western disciples, and TBMSG (Trailokya Bauddha Mahasangha Sahayak Gana), as the FWBO is known in India, is now a thriving and expanding part of the movement. Sangharakshita has written fascinating accounts of the first twelve years of his life in India in three volumes of memoirs.

Since his return to the West, he has given himself unstintingly to the work of spreading the Dharma, his greatest achievement being the foundation of a Buddhist movement that has successfully taken root in the conditions of secularized and industrialized Western civilization. FWBO centres now flourish in many countries, along with residential spiritual communities and 'Right Livelihood' businesses. Sangharakshita has also written prolifically, on Buddhism and related subjects.

In the last few years Sangharakshita has handed on most of his responsibilities to senior members of the Western Buddhist Order. He devotes most of his time to his literary work, but from time to time visits FWBO centres in different parts of the world.

Amitayus, detail
showing the flowering bowl

buddhism in
MINIATURE

THE UNSEEN FLOWER

Compassion is far more than emotion. It is something that springs
Up in the emptiness which is when you yourself are not there,
So that you do not know anything about it.
Nobody, in fact, knows anything about it
(If they knew it, it would not be Compassion);
But they can only smell
The scent of the unseen flower
That blooms in the Heart of the Void.

A Buddhist does not 'represent' Buddhism. If you represent Buddhism, you are not a Buddhist. A Buddhist *is* Buddhism – in miniature.

Aphorism

If you treat non-violence as the highest principle you can't go far wrong; so much follows from that. But, of course, non-violence isn't just a question of abstaining from killing and from eating meat. To follow the principle of non-violence is to be brought into the very heart of the spiritual life.

Q & A:
Tuscany 1981

The Priceless Jewel — Ever since the dawn of history … two great principles have been at work in the world: the principle of violence and the principle of non-violence or, as we may also call it, the principle of love…. The principle of violence is a principle of Darkness, the principle of non-violence a principle of Light. Whereas to live in accordance with the principle of violence is to be either an animal or a devil or a combination of the two, to live in accordance with the principle of non-violence is to be a human being, in the full sense of the term, or even an angel.

Correspondence — More and more I see the spiritual life in terms of learning to switch from the power mode to the love mode. If one can do that, everything else will follow.

To be a Buddhist in name only is worse than useless. A real Buddhist should change a little every day – should grow a little every day.

Correspondence

Religion cannot be taught; it can only be caught. You have to catch the spirit of religion, and you do that through the influence of other people.

Buddhism and Education. Lecture

Let us do away with the divisions between monastic and lay Buddhists, between men and women Buddhists, and between the followers of different sects and schools of Buddhism. Let us have an integrated Buddhism and an integrated Buddhist community. Let us base ourselves firmly and unmistakably upon our common Going for Refuge to the Buddha, the Dharma, and the Sangha.

Buddhism and the West

Correspondence Women should stop looking over their shoulders at men and trying to prove themselves equal to men. This does not mean that the sexes are unequal. It means that the concepts of equality and inequality are inappropriate. Women should simply do what is best for their own development as individuals without bothering about whether or not men are doing the same things or about where it leaves them in relation to men.

Correspondence To me it seems more obvious than ever that if we are to generate enough enthusiasm and inspiration to enable us to break through the bonds of our own individualism, as well as through the strongly anti-spiritual tendencies of modern life itself, we need the Bodhisattva Ideal. Only the Bodhisattva Ideal can carry us beyond ourselves and the world – and back again into them on a totally different basis.

If our deeper and more powerful emotions are still tied up with things of a worldly nature, our involvement with the Dharma can only be superficial, however sincere we may be. If we are to be truly Buddhist, our involvement with the Dharma must be truly passionate.

Correspondence

The whole criticism of religion as escapism is ridiculous. If you are suffering why shouldn't you get out? What's wrong with escaping? It's the sensible thing to do.

Seminar on the Udana

Correspondence The more deeply we get into the spiritual life the more our sense of reality changes. What seemed very real before now seems relatively unreal, and vice versa. Things seem more or less real according to the degree of our emotional investment in them. In any case, experiences – strange or otherwise – come and go, and we should not allow ourselves to become attached to them or even to take much interest in them. The main thing is to go on deepening our Going for Refuge in whatever way we can.

Aphorism Four basic propositions: (1) Man can change. (2) He can change himself. (3) He can help others to change. (4) Together they can change the world.

It is crucial to keep the transcendental element in Buddhism in mind. If you lose sight of that, you lose sight of Buddhism itself – and run the risk of getting bogged down in psychology.

Seminar on the Itivuttaka

Some people like Zen (so they say) because it is iconoclastic. They become quite upset, however, should anyone venture to be iconoclastic about Zen.

Aphorism

The more 'scholarly' a Buddhist is, the more firmly he needs to base himself on Going for Refuge, ethics, and meditation. Otherwise his influence may be disastrous.

Aphorism

*Seminar on the
Mahaparinibbana
Suttanta*

In order to reconcile Buddhism and Christianity you've got to know Buddhism and to know Christianity. You've got to be honest. You've got to be true to Buddhism and true to Christianity and reconcile the real Christianity with the real Buddhism. If you have an imaginary version of Christianity and an imaginary version of Buddhism, it might be easy to reconcile the two, but have you really reconciled Buddhism and Christianity? To do that you must know them really well; know them in depth; know them thoroughly. Only then might it be possible to suggest a framework vast enough to include them both – and that framework would have to be very vast indeed.

Aphorism

The only real advantage that Christianity has over Buddhism is that it is more poetic.

Buddhists are tolerant in the sense that they are able to differ profoundly from the followers of other religions on certain issues without regarding those followers with feelings of hostility, and without behaving violently towards them. Buddhist tolerance is not based on a belief in the oneness of all religions.

Correspondence

A spiritually barren period is not unusual in the life of even the most committed Buddhist. What is important is that we realize it is only a phase and wait for it to pass, and, in the meantime, do nothing that we may later on regret.

Correspondence

Guhyaloka Retreat Centre, Spain

a

LONG WAY
to go

UNPUBLISHED POEMS

'Every day is a good day': a thousand doors fly open.
'Every day is a good day': the sun and moon stand still.

The Blue Cliff rises high into the air;
Below it is wrapped in mist, above it is shrouded in cloud.
What use is a path up the sheer side,
If, however far you climb, you can never reach the top?

A hundred peaks behind, a hundred peaks before;
All at once, the Blue Cliff rises in the distance.
Birds disappear into the mist, monkeys' cries are lost in silence;
Darkness gathers, and there is still a long way to go.

For many people today morality amounts to not doing what we want to do, and doing what we do not want to do, because – for reasons we do not understand – we have been told to by someone in whose existence we no longer believe.

Vision and Transformation

Rest on your laurels and they will wither.

Aphorism

Strictly speaking there is no such thing as moral or spiritual stagnation. Contrary to what people usually think, stagnation is not a state in which, while things do not get any better, they at least do not get any worse. It is a state in which things get worse without our doing anything to make them worse.

Aphorism

Aphorism   Sometimes it is difficult to distinguish a temptation from an opportunity.

Seminar on the Sutra of Golden Light   It's much easier to deal with external pressures when there is no conflict within oneself. If you are relatively integrated, even when the whole of you is under pressure you have a better chance of resisting temptation. But if you've got a traitor within that is going to co-operate with the enemy without, you're in a much more difficult position.

Aphorism   It is a very dangerous thing to regard oneself as the instrument by which God, karma, or whatever, punishes other people. It could be called the Genghis Khan complex.

It is not that one is dishonest, but that one is only honest up to a point.

Aphorism

Never promise anything which it is not in your power to perform. That is, never promise anything for the performance of which you have to rely on other people.

Aphorism

We may have to leave our roots behind, in a sense, but it is a question of growing beyond them, not severing them abruptly by an act of will. I once wrote a poem entitled 'The Root Speaks'. Sometimes we have to listen to that Root.

Correspondence

Not everything that is legal is moral, and not everything that is illegal is immoral.

Aphorism

Seminar on the Way of Wisdom   Faith is the capacity for being emotionally moved – at least for the time being – by something that transcends the senses and even the rational mind.

Aphorism   If you won't get under the shower you can't complain if it isn't wetting you.

Correspondence   In a sense, to live from one day to the next requires a leap of faith, so it is hardly surprising that a step as momentous as committing oneself to the Three Jewels should require such a leap.

The hindrance of doubt isn't a sort of suspension of belief until such time as you have sufficient grounds to be able to make up your mind. Doubt is almost deliberately refusing to make up your mind – allowing yourself to be in a vacillating mental state, even, so that you will not have to commit yourself one way or the other.

Seminar on the Precious Garland

There is no doubt that spiritual development is sometimes a slow and painful process. It is not difficult to have 'insights' of a general kind, but it is very difficult to apply them to oneself.

Correspondence

Correspondence It is certainly possible to think of spiritual growth in terms of removing imperfections and becoming more pure, and many people find this approach helpful. But that does not justify dismissing the complementary method – trying to develop – as 'trying to make oneself into something else'. Both models have their limitations, and neither should be understood too literally.

Aphorism Humility is the pride of the weak.

We should modify the popular statement that one should 'accept oneself'. Dr Johnson defines the verb 'to accept' as 'to receive with approbation' – that is to say, with approval. But surely there is much in ourselves of which we do not approve, even much of which we strongly disapprove. We should not want to hang on to that, whatever it is. It would be better to say: 'Let us accept what is skilful in ourselves, but reject what is unskilful.' Indeed, without such an attitude, no spiritual development is possible.

Fifteen Points for Order Members. Lecture

Humiliation may even be counted amongst the ways in which Perfect Vision might arise – being cut down to size by reality itself – so it can be a very positive experience indeed. If you can take it as such, you find you can survive it. Life goes on. You pick yourself up, dust yourself down, and start all over again.

Wisdom Beyond Words

On the Opening of the Manchester Buddhist Centre. Lecture

We should not underestimate the role of the will in spiritual life. It is not enough to have feeling for the Buddha. We have to will to be like the Buddha. One might even say there is no spiritual life without will. Indeed, spiritual life could be defined as the constant willing of the good in all circumstances.

Seminar on the Sutra of Golden Light

One of the most important aspects of the spiritual life is that one should be aware of the consequences of one's own actions.

Many people experience themselves in a purely passive way, feeling that they are victims of circumstances. Sometimes the important thing is to *do* something: to experience your own energy, experience yourself in action. Otherwise you don't really feel alive. No real spiritual progress is possible until you start experiencing yourself as acting rather than acted upon.

Seminar on the Jewel Ornament of Liberation

Compromise is the enemy of the spiritual life, besides being psychologically undermining.

Correspondence

By itself, experiencing suffering doesn't teach one anything. If there has been no insight into the truth of suffering, one can very quickly forget, even if one has suffered a great deal. And, of course, insight into the truth of suffering can be gained even when one is happy.

Seminar on the Jewel Ornament of Liberation

Fifteen Points for Order Members. Lecture Try to make sure that the influences that are impinging on you are positive rather than negative. We may not be able to shut out all the input all the time, but we can be much more careful about what we choose to let in.

Seminar on the Sutra of Golden Light True confession is very important in the spiritual life, and very rare. In true confession there is no feeling of irrational guilt and no fear of rejection or any other form of punishment. On the contrary, one has complete trust in the person to whom one is making the confession, which means that one does not see him or her as an authority figure or as wielding any sort of 'power'. It is very difficult for a Westerner, and an ex-Christian, not to see the Buddha as God, i.e. as the embodiment of the power mode rather than of the love mode, and for this reason it is very difficult for a Western Buddhist to practise true confession and engage in true worship.

the courage of
POSITIVE EMOTIONS

Women from the Manchester Sangha

one's

THE STREAM OF STARS

The stream of my desire no more
Rolls through the muddy fields of earth;
Between the azure banks of heaven
A stream of stars has come to birth.

No more on my soul's current float
Dead leaves from wind-dishevelled trees;
But swanlike, many a shining boat
Bends low before the heavenly breeze.

The fountains of my heart no more
Ooze slow into some stagnant place,
But in great tranquil rivers pour
Into the boundless sea of space.

Wherever there is a wish to repeat an experience there is craving.

Aphorism

Buddhism distinguishes between *kamachanda*, 'worldly desire', and *dhammachanda*, 'spiritual desire'. So the aim is not to eliminate desire, but to eliminate craving.

Correspondence

A human being is a stream of consciousness deeply imbued with the dye of craving.

Seminar on the Dhammapada

Our everyday life may be pleasurable or painful; wildly ecstatic or unbearably agonizing; or just plain dull and boring much of the time. But it is here, in the midst of all these experiences, good, bad, and indifferent – and nowhere else – that Enlightenment is to be attained.

Wisdom Beyond Words

Seminar on the Jewel Ornament of Liberation

Some people, it seems, don't regard enjoyment as a natural thing. They almost have to teach themselves to enjoy life. André Gide, the French writer, had to discipline himself into enjoying the sun, the air, and the sea. It was quite an effort on his part.

If what we see is the utilitarian value·of something, we are relating to it from a need, which becomes desire, which turns to craving for the object conceived as fulfilling that desire. The tree is seen not as existing in its own right, for its own sake, but as something to fulfil our own need. If, however, we have no desires to be fulfilled, there is no subject and no object. That is the state of the Bodhisattva – empty of any desire to use things for any particular purpose. All that is left is aesthetic appreciation. If you are a Bodhisattva you enjoy the world much as you enjoy a work of art or an artistic performance – with the difference that you do not experience a division between yourself and something 'out there'.

Wisdom Beyond Words

Seminar on the Jewel Ornament of Liberation

Pleasure is a passive state, happiness an active one. We usually think of ourselves as lying back and enjoying happiness, but it isn't like that. We experience true happiness when we are active. And we are active when we meditate successfully, for then we are powerfully generating skilful mental states, and what can be more active – more creative – than that?

Seminar on the Precious Garland

The worldly-minded person thinks in terms of happiness, the spiritually-minded person thinks in terms of liberation.

Seminar on the Precious Garland

In the search for freedom, happiness is a by-product.

It has been said that Buddhism is an ascetic religion and this is very true. But it is ascetic in the original Greek sense of getting into training, to enable yourself to reach the goal of Enlightenment. You won't reach that goal if you are flabby or out of condition, spiritually speaking.

Seminar on the Nature of Existence

The more you enjoy life the more ascetic you will be, and the more ascetic you are, the more you'll enjoy life.

Seminar on the Nature of Existence

Happiness is to be irreversibly creative.

Seminar on the Nature of Existence

It's a bit ironic to talk about giving up worldly pleasures when you take up the spiritual life. It's much more like giving up worldly miseries and taking up spiritual happiness.

Seminar on the Samannaphala Sutta

The Veil of Stars.   It was desire that dashed from my hands the chalice that
Poem   love raised to my lips.

The Veil of Stars.   You can no more confine love within the limits of
Poem   human hearts
       Than you can catch the showering moonlight in cups of
       gold.

Aphorism   One can love people only as far as one understands
       them, and be ready to love them more when one
       understands them better.

It is better to establish real, living contact with our negative emotions (which means acknowledging them and experiencing them but not indulging them) than to remain in that alienated state and not experience our emotions at all.

A Guide to the Buddhist Path

Despite what the Dharma says, or is supposed to say, I don't think grief (*soka*) is invariably, under all circumstances, a negative (i.e. unskilful) state, though of course undue indulgence in grief is negative. In any case, no negative mental state should ever be repressed (repression being an unconscious process), as distinct from being consciously suppressed, in the sense of not being allowed to dominate the mind or to find inappropriate outward expression.

Correspondence

Aphorism Passivity is not to be mistaken for receptivity. The wet clay is not the open jar.

Correspondence It is often said that one should have the courage of one's convictions. Perhaps one should also have the courage of one's positive emotions.

Aphorism The only way to avoid hating one's fellow men is to love them.

Aphorism We only too often find it easier to hate the wicked than to love the good.

Love is no mere flabby sentiment but the vigorous expression of an imaginative identification with other living beings.

The Ten Pillars of Buddhism

Love is a self-giving of person to person, even a surrender of person to person – 'surrender' here meaning the complete abandonment of any advantage derived from the power mode.

The Ten Pillars of Buddhism

Personal development is not an easy matter for anyone, and there are times when we must bear with others, just as there are times when they must bear with us.

Correspondence

the heat of the
FURNACE

Chintamani working on
Manchester Buddhist Centre's Amitabha figure

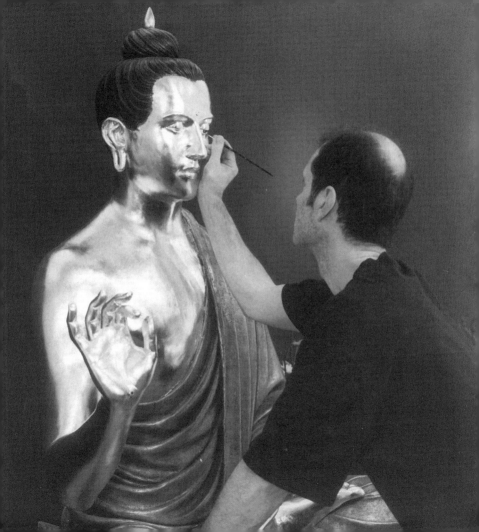

NEW

I should like to speak
With a new voice, speak
Like Adam in the Garden, speak
Like the Rishis of old, announcing
In strong jubilant voices the Sun
Moon Stars Dawn Winds Fire
Storm and above all the god-given
Intoxicating ecstatic
Soma, speak
Like divine men celebrating
The divine cosmos with divine names.
I should like to speak
With a new voice, telling
The new things that I know, chanting
In incomparable rhythms
New things to new men, singing

The new horizon, the new vision
The new dawn, the new day.
I should like to use
New words, use
Words pristine, primeval, words
Pure and bright as snow-crystals, words
Resonant, expressive, creative,
Such as, breathed to music, built Ilion.
(The old words
Are too tired soiled stale lifeless.)
New words
Come to me from the stars
From your eyes from
Space
New words vibrant, radiant, able to utter
The new me, able
To build for new
Men a new world.

Seminar on the Tibetan Book of the Dead

Culture is the preserved remains of what others before us have achieved, experienced, or discovered. By appreciating, understanding, and appropriating it we enrich our own lives and contribute to our own development.

Aphorism

Culture is a rainbow bridge thrown from the material world to the spiritual world.

The FWBO and 'Protestant Buddhism'

On finding itself in a Western environment, Buddhism has become the focus for an interaction between the timeless truths of the Dharma and the language of the secular Western culture through which it seeks to express those truths. Western Buddhism will be the creation of that interaction.

The fact that there is Buddhist culture does not necessarily mean that there is Buddhism, although there may be. Very often what people from the East bring to the West is Buddhist culture rather than Buddhism proper.

Seminar on the Precepts of the Gurus

Art is a means of overcoming alienation. We repossess ourselves of what we have lost by recreating it from within us.

Aphorism

Art is an object through which we find our way back to the subject.

Aphorism

The Religion of Art

Religious art is that kind of poetry, music, painting, or any other species of art, which conduces to the experience of egolessness. Much conventionally religious art ... is not religious art in this sense. It not only fails to induce the experience of egolessness, but even positively strengthens the ego-sense.

Seminar on the Tibetan Book of the Dead

The arts capture crude, egoistic energy and process it until it's more refined. It can then be utilized, so to speak, for the purposes of the spiritual life.

Aphorism

Religion has been defined as what a man does with his solitude. Art might be similarly defined.

Aesthetic appreciation is pure delight in the object of contemplation for its own sake. This is the difference between lust, which is stimulated by the sensuously attractive, and the aesthetic sense, which is stimulated by pure beauty. If you look with craving, you see things in terms of sensuous attractiveness, but if you look with metta, with loving kindness, you see things in terms of beauty. Metta is disinterested. When it's a question of lust you want to grab; when it's a question of aesthetic appreciation, you just want to stand back and contemplate.

*Seminar on the
Precious Garland*

Only too often people think the poets do not mean what they say. They think it is 'just poetry'. The poets, however, mean *exactly* what they say.

Aphorism

Aphorism   One of the signs of a great writer is that even his bad work is interesting – more interesting than the best work of a mediocre writer.

Aphorism   Every creative writer is the founder of a new religion.

Aphorism   The fact that an author is dissatisfied with his work does not mean that the critics have the right to be.

Aphorism   One does not write a book. One writes sentences.

Aphorism   Writing memoirs is the penance one performs for having lived – or not lived.

The writer invites you to read his book, the artist to look at his painting; the religious teacher invites you to share his life.

Aphorism

When poetry is no longer enjoyed it ceases to be poetry – at least for the one reading it or listening to it.

Aphorism

With so many masterpieces of world literature to read it is a pity to waste one's time on trivia. Indeed, it is a pity to waste one's time on anything that does not genuinely enhance the quality of one's life, that does not deepen one's positive emotions – that does not, in short, help one to become enlightened.

Correspondence

Correspondence Speaking personally, I never show what I am writing to anybody, and never discuss it. I do not even really like to be asked how I am 'getting on with my writing'. Authorship is an essentially solitary business, and any outside interference, whether from government censors or well-meaning friends, is rightly to be resented.

Aphorism Diaries can be very misleading – especially when they contain nothing but facts.

Correspondence Creative writing in the true sense is a spiritual discipline that calls for the same kind of seriousness and dedication as the spiritual life itself.

At the moment of the creation of a work of art, the feelings experienced may be very intense and powerful. They may come welling up from the depths quite uncontrollably. Should anything get in your way, or should there be any sort of interruption or disturbance, you can react quite violently, just because you are so absorbed in what you are doing. In the process of artistic creation you are bringing together into a unity a whole mass of materials, by virtue of the intensity of your feelings, even of your Insight, and great psychic pressure is needed to do that. Milton's artistic inspiration has been described as being like a great furnace which he kept banking up until it was just a mass of glowing coals. Into it he flung all sorts of things – his knowledge, all the materials he had gathered – but such was the heat of the furnace that he could melt down all those materials and cast them into a mould of his own.

Seminar on the Jewel Ornament of Liberation

Correspondence What we need is a new generation of writers and artists who are committed to the spiritual life, as well as dedicated to their particular art, and for whom the former inspires the latter while the latter provides the former with a means of expression. This is, of course, something much more subtle than simply using the arts as a vehicle of religious propaganda.

Correspondence The written word remains. Even the noblest actions and the wisest utterances are known to us only by their being – eventually – written down.

Correspondence Writing is no substitute for face-to-face communication – unless one can write a whole book.

Cultivate an aphorism as you would cultivate a rose; but be careful not to remove the thorns.

Aphorism

Sometimes we use words very loosely and inaccurately, because we do not ask ourselves what they mean. Our speech is laden with jargon from various sources, and that does not conduce to clarity. So let us understand the meaning of the words we speak, and especially the words we write, consulting the dictionary if necessary. The most useful book in the world, I think, leaving aside the scriptures, is the dictionary.

Fifteen Points for Order Members. Lecture

I plead for a greater, more vivid realization of the poetic nature of speech. This should be our approach to language all the time, because language, as applied to non-material realities, is essentially metaphorical, poetry rather than prose.

Q & A on the Jewel Ornament of Liberation

Wisdom Beyond
Words

In metaphor language begins to transcend itself.
Metaphor offers us a clue to the nature of reality.

Q & A:
Tuscany 1984

Language – even abstract language – is essentially
metaphorical. Of course, one can ask how, if this is so,
words can describe reality. But that assumes that reality
is not metaphorical, that it is somehow abstract, as
science usually thinks of it. But if language *is*
metaphorical, this suggests that reality too is
metaphorical, and that one can get closer to reality by
realizing that language is metaphorical.

Nursery run by Indian Buddhists
in the Poona slums

the real
REVOLUTIONARY

I WANT TO BREAK OUT

I want to break out,
Batter down the door,
Go tramping black heather all day
On the windy moor,
And at night, in hayloft, or under hedge, find
A companion suited to my mind.

I want to break through,
Shatter time and space,
Cut up the Void with a knife,
Pitch the stars from their place,
Nor shrink back when, lidded with darkness, the Eye
Of Reality opens and blinds me, blue as the sky.

Children aren't just members of the family; they are eventually going to be members of society. They have to be brought up to consider other people's feelings and respect other people's property.

Fifteen Points for Buddhist Parents. Lecture

One of the most important things we can teach our children is to empathize with others – with other children, with animals, with all living beings. Otherwise their recognition of the distinction between right and wrong will be purely theoretical.

Fifteen Points for Buddhist Parents. Lecture

Parents will always be deeply affected by anything that concerns their children, whether for good or ill; but we have to try to remain detached, without losing our human feelings. In fact we should try to universalize our feelings, and feel as much for our neighbour's child as for our own.

Correspondence

Buddhism and Education. Lecture

The first purpose of education is to enable the individual to take his place as a functioning, responsible member of the wider society to which he belongs.

New Currents in Western Buddhism

The group is a collectivity organized for its own survival, in which the interests of the individual are subordinated to those of the collectivity. The group is also a power-structure in which the ultimate sanction is force.

Correspondence

Group attitudes die very hard.

The Priceless Jewel

The truly human, consciously evolving individual is characterized by awareness, emotional positivity, responsibility, intelligence, creativity, spontaneity, imagination, and insight.

The Buddha's teaching is concerned solely with the individual, both alone and in free association with other individuals. It shows the individual how to grow, shows him or her, by means of actual methods, how to develop awareness and emotional positivity, how to live spontaneously and creatively, how to accept responsibility for oneself and for others. Gautama the Buddha, the original teacher, was and is an example of a true individual. Indeed, he was an individual of the truest kind: an Enlightened individual.

New Currents in Western Buddhism

If one is healthy, one has energy, and if one has energy, one naturally wants to put it into something – that is, one wants to work, whether the work consists in digging the soil or painting a picture.

Correspondence

Correspondence   Without unremitting effort nothing truly great is ever achieved. All the great artists seem to have been great workers. Perhaps this was because they loved their work.

Correspondence   Sometimes I think work – real work, work in which one believes – is the greatest enjoyment in life.

Correspondence   Work should be an expression of one's life, not simply the means to one's existence.

Aphorism   'A load of sandalwood is still a load,' said the camel.

Much of what is thought of as history is really myth. Not *Aphorism*
that it is necessarily any the worse for that, of course, but
it would be better if things were called by their right
names.

Though rights and duties are reciprocal, one should *Seminar on*
place the emphasis on one's duties rather than on one's *the Duties of*
Brotherhood in
rights. If you faithfully discharge your duties, the *Islam*
chances are that other people will observe their duties
towards you, and you will in fact get your rights. If there
is a mutual recognition of duties, there is no need to
speak of rights at all. Other factors being equal, people
start claiming their rights only when other people have
been very remiss in the performance of their duties.

Rights exist only within the group: within the spiritual *Aphorism*
community there are only duties.

Q & A:
Tuscany 1982   From a Buddhist point of view, your duty is what you
see as incumbent upon yourself in view of the principles
in which you believe, and the situation in which you find
yourself.

Crossing the
Stream   The remedy for any injustice or inequality in human
relationships, whether domestic, social, civic, political,
cultural, racial, or religious, is an insistence not upon the
rights of one party, but on the duties of the other.

Aphorism   Formerly one needed courage to attack institutions. Now
one needs courage to defend them – and still more
courage to create them.

It is not on ideological grounds that one tries to break down class barriers. One tries to break them down simply because one wants to be able to relate to other people as individuals.

Q & A:
Tuscany 1982

Liberalism is the belief that life should be fair. Pseudo-liberalism is the belief that fairness can be achieved by unfair means.

Aphorism

Equality is a concept that has a place only in arithmetic.

Aphorism

Inequality is life. Equality is death.

Aphorism

A good man sometimes helps to perpetuate a bad system, and vice versa.

Aphorism

Correspondence   The larger society needs to have a set of shared values, in however dilute a form. Otherwise it could not cohere – could not be a society at all. At the same time, there is little doubt that the truly ideal society could exist only on a small scale, in a number of different embodiments within the larger society.

Correspondence   'Political correctness' is one of the most pernicious tendencies of our time – far more pernicious than pseudo-liberalism, of which it is probably the extreme form.

Q & A:
Tuscany 1982   It would seem that there will always be a minority of people in society who will try to harm others. The majority will therefore need to invoke force, at least to restrain them from their anti-social conduct. I don't think one can get round that.

It is in the interests of Buddhists to work wherever possible for a pluralistic society; a threat to any minority is a threat to Buddhism. But for there to be a pluralistic society, the adherents of the religions and other ideologies which exist within that society must recognize the possibility, even the desirability, of their peaceful coexistence. That does imply a certain common ethical outlook, certain ethical values, such as the ideal of tolerance, or the spirit of live and let live.

Q & A on the Noble Eightfold Path

If everyone bears his or her full share of responsibility, there will be no room for authoritarianism. Unfortunately, people criticize others for authoritarianism while at the same time they are reluctant to recognize their own responsibility within a given situation. They want others to accept all or most of the responsibility, and do all or most of the work; at the same time, they want to be able to control those others.

Correspondence

Seminar on the
Sevenfold Puja

It is sometimes said: 'There is no revolutionary like an old revolutionary.' The young revolutionary is just hot-blooded, just impulsive, and usually he gets over it and settles down and conforms, but the real revolutionary is one who, the older he gets, the more revolutionary he gets.

Meditation, Cambridge Buddhist Centre

no last-minute

METHODS

MEDITATION

Here perpetual incense burns;
The heart to meditation turns,
And all delights and passions spurns.

A thousand brilliant hues arise,
More lovely than the evening skies,
And pictures paint before our eyes.

All the spirit's storm and stress
Is stilled into a nothingness,
And healing powers descend and bless.

Refreshed, we rise and turn again
To mingle with this world of pain,
As on roses falls the rain.

'All worldlings are mad,' said the Buddha, and in the long run a mad person may do anything. Hence the importance of developing insight into reality.

Correspondence

There are no last-minute methods. Since one is, in principle, facing death every minute, all insight meditation practices are methods of 'coping' with the problem of death and consequently with the fear of death. At times when death seems near one should therefore do whatever practice one is most familiar with, or has most faith in. One should be careful not to relax one's efforts when the crisis has passed, or appears to have passed, which is what usually happens.

Correspondence

Meditation is essentially the willing of the Good.

Aphorism

Correspondence Without regular meditation, our spiritual life has no sheet anchor.

Mind – Reactive and Creative The optimism of the creative mind persists despite unpleasant stimuli…. [It] loves where there is no reason to love, is happy where there is no reason for happiness, creates where there is no possibility of creativity, and in this way 'builds a heaven in hell's despair'.

Correspondence Most people either repress fear completely or allow it to diffuse itself throughout the whole of their experience in the form of a vague feeling of anxiety or dread. But fear is inseparable from one's consciousness of oneself as a separate individual. As one advances in the spiritual life, and especially as one practises meditation, one is sure to have to face it.

As what we fear approaches, we realize it is not really this that we are afraid of after all. What it is that we are afraid of, we do not know.

Aphorism

Logic is a highly irrational phenomenon.

Aphorism

Reason must be supreme in all human affairs, say the Rationalists. But on what grounds do they accept the truth of this statement? If it is on authority, reason is not supreme; if on rational grounds, then they assume the supremacy of reason in order to establish the supremacy of reason.

Aphorism

A philosophy cannot be founded on reasons.

Aphorism

A Guide to the
Buddhist Path

The development of positive emotions ... is absolutely crucial to our development as individuals. It is, after all, our emotions which keep us going; we are not kept going by abstract ideas. It is our positive emotions which keep us going on the spiritual path, giving us inspiration, enthusiasm, and so on, until such time as we can develop Perfect Vision [i.e. vipashyana or Insight] and be motivated by that.

Correspondence

The problem of how to combine reason and emotion, so that we think what we feel and feel what we think, at ever higher levels, is one that all who are concerned with personal development have to face sooner or later. In their most developed forms, reason is vipashyana or insight and emotion is shamatha or calm – though by that stage of development they have already begun to coincide.

'External understanding' is an understanding which is
not part of yourself, which is dissoclated from yourself.
It is that alienated intellect which in Blake's symbolism
is represented by the figure of Urizen. Not only is one
not able to understand the Buddha's teaching with
alienated intellect: one can't understand anything with it.
From Blake's point of view the whole of modern science
is an attempt to understand life by the alienated intellect.

*Seminar on the
Heartfelt Advice
to Rechungpa*

Unless your alienated intellect is transformed by being
brought into contact with very strong emotion so that the
two are fused, there is no possibility of developing
Insight. Insight is no nearer to intellect than it is to
emotion.

*Seminar on the
Heartfelt Advice
to Rechungpa*

Seminar on Outlines of Mahayana Buddhism
When we get on to the spiritual path, the conflict between the rational and the emotional has been virtually resolved, so that you have a sort of unified energy, still mundane but unified, and orientated in the direction of the transcendental.

Correspondence
It is true that one needs to unify one's energy. But if one's energy is not unified one should not worry about it, otherwise energy will be wasted in worrying and unification will be further away than ever.

Aphorism
Positive emotion is emotion which is pleasurable and at the same time skilful.

Only when a man feels strongly will he act effectively. It is for this reason above all others that Buddhism starts not with a concept but with a feeling, not with intellectual postulation but with emotional experience.

Crossing the Stream

Padmavajra and Surata.
Padmaloka Retreat Centre

FRIENDSHIP &
communication

FOUR GIFTS

I come to you with four gifts.
The first gift is a lotus-flower.
Do you understand?
My second gift is a golden net.
Can you recognize it?
My third gift is a shepherds' round-dance.
Do your feet know how to dance?
My fourth gift is a garden planted in a wilderness.
Could you work there?
I come to you with four gifts.
Dare you accept them?

Nowadays people don't have friends; they have psychotherapists, lawyers, and hairdressers.

Aphorism

Spiritual fellowship is indeed the whole of the spiritual life, as well as being the panacea for ordinary psychological problems.

Correspondence

True competition is a form of collaboration.

Aphorism

'Take rhetoric and wring its neck', said the French poet. Charisma, one might add, is the psychological equivalent of rhetoric.

Aphorism

Correspondence   'Joviality' sometimes masks competitiveness and even antagonism. Thus it is the near enemy of mudita (sympathetic joy).

Correspondence   Friendship is certainly a vital part of Buddhism, but non-exclusiveness is equally a vital part of friendship.

Correspondence   Our real friends are indeed people who welcome us with a warm hug however long we have been away, and who are not interested in what they can get out of us for themselves. Such friends are Bodhisattvas in the form of ordinary human beings, as Gampopa calls them.

Correspondence   Friendships must certainly be kept up. They can't look after themselves, or be kept in cold storage.

The emotions connected with friendship are skilful but weak; the emotions connected with sex are unskilful but strong. The former therefore need to be cultivated, the latter gradually eliminated.

Aphorism

A sexual relationship is like a lobster pot – easy to get into but difficult to get out of.

Aphorism

Without chastity it is difficult to experience spiritual androgyny, and without the experience of spiritual androgyny it is difficult to achieve a vision of the Truth.

Aphorism

It is difficult to know which is worse: not to be believed when you speak the truth, or to be believed when you tell a lie.

Aphorism

Aphorism Not to be believed means to be cut off from communication. It means to be treated as an object.

Correspondence The Enlightenment experience is not self-contained in a one-sided way. It contains an element of communication and therefore an element of spiritual friendship, even transcendental friendship – friendship on the highest conceivable level.

The primary meaning of *kalyana* in kalyana mitrata (spiritual friendship) is 'beautiful'. In spiritual friendship we take delight in the spiritual beauty of our dear friend. This aspect of 'taking delight' means that we not only see a person as a person, but also like what we see, enjoy and take delight in what we see, just as we do with a beautiful painting or poem – except that here the painting or poem is alive: the painting can speak to you, and the beautiful poem can answer back. This makes it very exciting and stimulating indeed.

Correspondence

It is appalling to think how much time, energy, and initiative it takes to get to know even one person very well.

Correspondence

A fool can give more advice in a day than a wise man can follow in a year.

Aphorism

Aphorism   It seems extraordinary that people should have such difficulty understanding what seems to be a straightforward point. Perhaps it is because they are thinking of something else.

Correspondence   Things that are allowed to remain unspoken eventually build up an insurmountable barrier to communication. Either one communicates or one is blocked. There is no middle way.

Correspondence   'Manner' is such an elusive thing. Different people can perceive a person's manner in quite different ways and therefore have quite different reactions to it. So, it is usually better to pay attention to the substance of someone's communication, not to its manner.

Speaking personally, I do not want disciples who are meek and obedient and afraid to speak their mind. I want disciples who are bold, self-confident, and independent and who are capable of standing against the whole world if necessary.

Correspondence

In spiritual life there will always be ups and downs, and during the down periods our spiritual friends are our main source of help and inspiration.

Correspondence

We have to try to appreciate people's positive qualities, without dwelling on their weaknesses.

Correspondence

Correspondence   Criticism is not condemnation. Personally I never condemn anyone, since I believe that human beings are capable of change. Criticism, if taken in the right spirit, helps us to grow.

Correspondence   Don't be impatient, especially with other people. Realize that sometimes they have their problems too. Though they may want to be friends, in practice they may find it difficult. Try not to think in terms of what other people should be giving you, but rather in terms of what you can give them.

Conversation   When people make you more than human they in effect make you less than human. The only important thing is for us to be friends; and whatever teaching is to happen will come over naturally in the course of the friendship.

Few are great enough to serve.

Aphorism

Authoritarianism and spiritual life are completely incompatible. Most 'gurus' are simply exploiters.

Correspondence

If in each generation the disciples fall below the level of attainment of the guru, in a few generations what's going to be the state of affairs? So a guru should consider that he has not been successful as a guru until his disciples do better than himself. Otherwise the chances are that the whole tradition will degenerate very quickly.

Seminar on the Heartfelt Advice to Rechungpa

Correspondence   It is sometimes necessary to criticize the weaknesses of others, but people often seem to find it difficult to do so without doing it in a 'hard' sort of way that excludes compassion. Perhaps, in some cases, people criticize others as a way of paying homage to the ideal without actually having to practise that ideal.

Correspondence   As Buddhists, we have to learn to live, work, and communicate together on the basis of our common commitment to the Three Jewels, without attaching too much importance to differences which are, after all, only part of our general psychological and social conditioning.

One of the great disadvantages of the mass-media is that trivialities can be given an importance that they absolutely don't possess. People need to be delivered not just from tragedy and disaster, but from triviality. Triviality, in fact, is one of the greatest disasters that can happen to us.

Q & A: WBO Convention 1985

Where there is trust, explanations are unnecessary. Where there is no trust, explanations are useless.

Aphorism

Sound judgement is a very rare quality. People do not necessarily possess it because they are sincere and well-meaning and spiritually committed, or because they have one's interests (where it is a question of giving personal advice) genuinely at heart. In refusing to accept someone's judgements one is not, therefore, questioning their integrity or their spiritual development.

Correspondence

Correspondence   There is no time in life for misunderstandings.

Aphorism   If you do not wear your heart on your sleeve for daws to peck at, the daws will accuse you of having no heart.

Fifteen Points for Order Members. Lecture   Don't argue. Discuss. When you get into an argument, what you are concerned with is to win, to beat the other person. But the aim of discussion is to find out between you the truth of the matter. If you are not very careful, what starts off as a genuine discussion can become an argument.

The Veil of Stars. Poem   There is no wound that man can give
That nature cannot heal.

To understand all is perhaps to forgive all. But
sometimes we have to forgive without understanding.

Aphorism

One of the problems facing the religious teacher is that
literal-minded people want literal answers to literal
questions.

Aphorism

Fooling other people can be dangerous, but fooling
oneself is fatal.

Aphorism

Head of a Bodhisattva,
Tuquz-Sarai, fifth century CE

the circle of
ETERNITY

ABOVE ME BROODS

Above me broods
A world of mysteries and magnitudes.
I see, I hear,
More than what strikes the eye or meets the ear.

Within me sleep
Potencies deep, unfathomably deep,
Which, when awake,
The bonds of life, death, time and space will break.

Infinity
Above me like the blue sky do I see.
Below, in me,
Lies the reflection of infinity.

If one always tries to explain the unknown by the known *Aphorism*
one will never learn anything.

Beware of premature syntheses. *Aphorism*

Only those who experience death in life can experience *Aphorism*
life in death.

The fundamental principle of my philosophy is that *Aphorism*
power and value do not coincide.

A perfect sphere on a perfect plane: are they or are they *Aphorism*
not in contact?

Aphorism   Time is unable to square the circle of eternity.

Aphorism   Security is insecurity. 'That which is supported has no support.'

Aphorism   A white dot against a black background: how does one tell whether it is revolving or stationary?

Aphorism   Soul is reticulated into souls.

Aphorism   It is not that there are two worlds which, while distinct, equally have ontological status. The distinction is between the ontological and the —?

Change your consciousness and you will see a different world. Change your consciousness and you will see the world differently. What is the difference between these two statements?

Aphorism

Intellectual clarity is not everything, but it counts for a great deal, especially when one remembers that Right View constitutes a basis for the development of Perfect Vision.

Correspondence

Correspondence Perhaps dreams have no explanation in the ordinary sense. They are their own explanation. Probably the best thing one can do is reflect upon the images of which the dream consists and try to retain and intensify the distinctive emotional quality of the dream experience. The dream, after all, is you, though a part of yourself which you do not usually experience, and with which you need, perhaps, to be more in touch.

A Survey of Buddhism To distinguish between thoughts and things, between the concepts which merely indicate realities and those realities themselves, is an art belonging to a highly advanced stage of philosophical discipline and spiritual culture.

'There is nothing in the mind that was not previously in the senses.' If this were true, the recollection of former lives would be impossible.

Aphorism

The Pali scriptures speak of multiple consciousnesses associated with single bodies, besides the more usual one consciousness to one body. I suppose that in this area, as in so many others, we have to beware of thinking too much in terms of fixed patterns, and be open to the possibility of there being patterns different from those with which we are familiar.

Correspondence

There can be no absolute duality between dualism and non-dualism. The absolute truth is the absolute truth of the relative truth. They are inseparable.

Wisdom Beyond Words

Seminar on the Nature of Existence

The doctrine of 'no-self' represents the possibility of change, radical change – change from reactive to creative, conditioned to unconditioned, mundane to transcendental.

Seminar on the Nature of Existence

Thought is incommensurable with reality and reality with thought.

SOURCES

SEMINARS BY SANGHARAKSHITA:

Unpublished seminar on *The Dhammapada* trans. Sangharakshita (unpublished)

Unpublished seminar on 'The Heartfelt Advice to Rechungpa' from *The 100,000 Songs of Milarepa*, trans. G.C.C. Chang (Shambhala, Boulder 1977)

Unpublished seminar on 'The Itivuttaka' from *The Minor Anthologies of the Pali Canon, part II*, trans. F.L. Woodward (OUP, London 1948)

Unpublished seminar on *The Jewel Ornament of Liberation* by Gampopa, trans. H.V. Guenther (Rider, London 1959)

Unpublished seminar on 'The Mahaparinibbana Suttanta' from *Dialogues of the Buddha, part II*, trans. T.W. Rhys Davids (Luzac, London 1971)

Unpublished seminar on *Outlines of Mahayana Buddhism* by D.T. Suzuki (Rider, London 1963)

Unpublished seminar on 'The Precepts of the Gurus', from W.Y.
Evans-Wentz, *Tibetan Yoga and Secret Doctrines* (OUP,
Oxford 1960)

Unpublished seminar on *The Precious Garland* by Nagarjuna, trans.
Jeffrey Hopkins and Lati Rimpoche (George Allen and Unwin,
London 1975)

Unpublished seminar on 'The Nature of Existence' from
Sangharakshita, *The Three Jewels* (Windhorse, Glasgow 1991)

Unpublished seminar on 'The Samannaphala Sutta', from A.A.G.
Bennett, *Long Discourses of the Buddha (Digha Nikaya)* (Chetana,
Bombay n.d.)

Unpublished seminar on *The Sevenfold Puja* compiled by
Sangharakshita (Windhorse, Glasgow 1990)

Unpublished seminar on *The Sutra of Golden Light*, trans.
R.E. Emmerick (Pali Text Society, London 1979)

Unpublished seminar on *The Tibetan Book of The Dead*, trans.
W.Y. Evans-Wentz (OUP, London 1972)

Unpublished seminar on 'The Udana' from *The Minor Anthologies of
the Pali Canon, part II*, trans. F.L. Woodward (OUP, London 1948)

Unpublished seminar on 'The Way of Wisdom' by E. Conze, from *The
Wheel, vol.iv* (Buddhist Publication Society, Kandy 1980)

Unpublished seminar on *The Duties of Brotherhood in Islam* by
Al Ghazali, trans. Muhtar Holland (Islamic Text Foundation,
Leicester 1975)

Questions and Answers on Sangharakshita's lecture series 'The Noble
Eightfold Path' published as *Vision and Transformation* (Windhorse,
Glasgow 1990)

LECTURES BY SANGHARAKSHITA:

'Fifteen Points for Order Members (Old and New)', London 1993

'Buddhism and Education', Bombay 1982

'Fifteen Points for Buddhist Parents', London 1994

'On the Opening of the Manchester Buddhist Centre', Manchester 1996

The talks above that were delivered in London are available from
DHARMACHAKRA TAPES, P.O. BOX 50, CAMBRIDGE, CB1 3BG

BOOKS BY SANGHARAKSHITA:

Buddhism and the West, Windhorse 1992
Complete Poems 1941–1994, Windhorse 1995
Crossing the Stream, Windhorse 1996
The FWBO and 'Protestant Buddhism', Windhorse 1992
A Guide to the Buddhist Path, Windhorse 1996
Mind – Reactive and Creative, Windhorse 1995
New Currents in Western Buddhism, Windhorse 1990
The Priceless Jewel, Windhorse 1993
The Religion of Art, Windhorse 1988
A Survey of Buddhism, Windhorse 1993
The Ten Pillars of Buddhism, Windhorse 1996
Vision and Transformation, Windhorse 1990
Wisdom Beyond Words, Windhorse 1993

The above are available from

WINDHORSE PUBLICATIONS
11 PARK ROAD
MOSELEY
BIRMINGHAM
B13 8AB   UK

WINDHORSE PUBLICATIONS INC
540 SOUTH 2ND WEST
MISSOULA
MT 59802
USA

ILLUSTRATIONS

The Windhorse symbolizes the energy of the enlightened mind carrying the Three Jewels – the Buddha, the Dharma, and the Sangha – to all sentient beings.

Buddhism is one of the fastest growing spiritual traditions in the Western world. Throughout its 2,500-year history, it has always succeeded in adapting its mode of expression to suit whatever culture it has encountered.

Windhorse Publications aims to continue this tradition as Buddhism comes to the West. Today's Westerners are heirs to the entire Buddhist tradition, free to draw instruction and inspiration from all the many schools and branches. Windhorse publishes works by authors who not only understand the Buddhist tradition but are also familiar with Western culture and the Western mind.

For orders and catalogues contact

WINDHORSE PUBLICATIONS
11 PARK ROAD
MOSELEY
BIRMINGHAM
B13 8AB   UK

WINDHORSE PUBLICATIONS INC
540 SOUTH 2ND WEST
MISSOULA
MT 59802
USA

Windhorse Publications is an arm of the Friends of the Western Buddhist Order, which has more than forty centres on four continents. Through these centres, members of the Western Buddhist Order offer regular programmes of events for the general public and for more experienced students. These include meditation classes, public talks, study on Buddhist themes and texts, and 'bodywork' classes such as t'ai chi, yoga, and massage. The FWBO also runs several retreat centres and the Karuna Trust, a fundraising charity that supports social welfare projects in the slums and villages of India.

Many FWBO centres have residential spiritual communities and ethical businesses associated with them. Arts activities are encouraged too, as is the development of strong bonds of friendship between people who share the same ideals. In this way the FWBO is developing a unique approach to Buddhism, not simply as a set of techniques, less still as an exotic cultural interest, but as a creatively directed way of life for people living in the modern world.

If you would like more information about the FWBO please write to

LONDON BUDDHIST CENTRE	**ARYALOKA**
51 ROMAN ROAD	**HEARTWOOD CIRCLE**
LONDON	**NEWMARKET**
E2 0HU UK	**NH 03857 USA**

ALSO FROM WINDHORSE

SANGHARAKSHITA
COMPLETE POEMS 1941–1994

Sangharakshita has dedicated himself to helping people transform their lives not only through his work as a Buddhist teacher but also through the medium of verse, for in his poetry he combines the sensitivity of the poet with the vision born of a life of contemplation and uncompromising spiritual practice.

Here we have the opportunity to listen to a unique voice and to be uplifted by the reflections of an extraordinary person and an accomplished teacher.

528 pages, hardback
ISBN 0 904766 70 5
£17.99/$34.95

SANGHARAKSHITA
PEACE IS A FIRE

This collection of aphorisms, teachings, and poems by the pioneering
Western Buddhist Sangharakshita offers instant inspiration to anyone
who is ready to have their views challenged and their minds expanded.

   The breadth of the author's thought is well represented in these
sayings which range from art and literature, through sex and
relationships, to philosophy and religion. His words point beyond
themselves to Reality itself, to the freedom accessible to all who dare to
change.

160 pages, with photographs
ISBN 0 904766 84 5
£6.99/$13.95

SANGHARAKSHITA
WHAT IS THE DHARMA?
THE ESSENTIAL TEACHINGS OF THE BUDDHA

Guided by a lifetime's experience of Buddhist practice, Sangharakshita tackles the question 'What is the Dharma?' from many different angles. The result is a basic starter kit of teachings and practices, which emphasizes the fundamentally practical nature of Buddhism.

In turn refreshing, unsettling, and inspiring, this book lays before us the essential Dharma, timeless and universal: the Truth that addresses the deepest questions of our hearts and minds and the Path that shows us how we can renew our lives.

272 pages, illustrated
ISBN 0 899579 01 X
£9.99/$19.95

KAMALASHILA

MEDITATION:
THE BUDDHIST WAY OF TRANQUILLITY AND INSIGHT

A comprehensive guide to the methods and theory of Buddhist meditation, written in an informal, accessible style. It provides a complete introduction to the basic techniques, as well as detailed advice for more experienced meditators seeking to deepen their practice.

The author is a long-standing member of the Western Buddhist Order, and has been teaching meditation since 1975. In 1979 he helped to establish a semi-monastic community in North Wales, which has now grown into a public retreat centre. For more than a decade he and his colleagues developed approaches to meditation that are firmly grounded in Buddhist tradition but readily accessible to people with a modern Western background. Their experience – as meditators, as students of the traditional texts, and as teachers – is distilled in this book.

304 pages, with charts and illustrations
ISBN 1 899579 05 2
£12.99/$25.95

SANGHARAKSHITA

A GUIDE TO THE BUDDHIST PATH

Which Buddhist teachings really matter? How does one begin to practise them in a systematic way? Without a guide one can easily get dispirited or lost.

In this highly readable anthology a leading Western Buddhist sorts out fact from myth, essence from cultural accident, to reveal the fundamental ideals and teachings of Buddhism. The result is a reliable map of the Buddhist path that anyone can follow.

Sangharakshita is an ideal companion on the path. As founder of a major Western Buddhist movement he has helped thousands of people to make an effective contact with the richness and beauty of the Buddha's teachings.

256 pages, with illustrations
ISBN 1 899579 04 4
£12.50/$24.95

PARAMANANDA
**CHANGE YOUR MIND:
A PRACTICAL GUIDE TO BUDDHIST MEDITATION**

Buddhism is based on the truth that, with effort, we can change the way
we are. But how? Among the many methods Buddhism has to offer,
meditation is the most direct. It is the art of getting to know one's own
mind and learning to encourage what is best in us.

This is an accessible and thorough guide to meditation, based on
traditional material but written in a light and modern style. Colourfully
illustrated with anecdotes and tips from the author's experience as a
meditator and teacher, it also offers refreshing inspiration to seasoned
meditators.

208 pages, with photographs
ISBN 0 904766 81 0
£8.50/$16.95